Speaking Hearts

© 2018 Ellen L. Pfaff

Speaking Hearts
2nd edition

ISBN-10: 1-946702-13-7

ISBN-13: 978-1-946702-13-5

Freeze Time Media

Speaking Hearts

Compiled by Ellen L. Pfaff

Acknowledgments

I want to thank all my family and friends for helping and being so patient with me through this very special project. I also want to thank all the teachers and students who have contributed their thoughts and feelings into these poems and letters.

I especially want to thank my children, Kristy, Eddie, and Andy, for giving me their love and support. For helping me through the rough times and for being there when I needed them.

Contents

INTRODUCTION   IX

DEAR MOM & DAD   1

LOST LOVE   21

A SPECIAL WAY TO SAY I LOVE YOU   53

FAMILY   85

Introduction

When I started to write "Speaking Hearts," my intent was to let children and adults know that they are not alone. I have found that many people have something to say to someone, but for whatever reason, can't seem to say what's in their hearts. It's been my experience that children seem to suffer from this problem more than adults do. This problem seems to occur more often to children who have lived with divorce, separations, or even the death of a parent. These children seem to have a lot to say, but don't really have anyone to listen to them. Instead, they keep these feelings inside and sometimes release it through bad behavior or they're not able to release it at all.

I have three children that I have raised on my own for the last 10 years. Over the years, they have built up resentment towards their father, and now he is almost a stranger to them. They missed out on the closeness and guidance that a father usually gives his children freely. I know my sons have really missed the male bonding, having a male figure to talk to about problems that they can't or don't feel comfortable talking to me about. My daughter, who is 20 years old now, has always found it very helpful to put her feelings down in a poem. She had written a poem about her father called "Daddy, can you hear me?" This poem shows the pain and hurt she feels towards her father.

In my case, my children are not able to tell their father how they feel when they are face-to-face with him. They aren't comfortable enough to talk to him about their feelings and end up either being silent or giving him an awkward smile when he asked what's on their minds. Since they don't see him on a daily basis and don't have the closeness, they are afraid to rock the boat or say anything that might hurt his feelings, for fear that he will completely abandon them.

Sometimes adults don't realize what kind of damage they can do to their children when they abandon them in their early years. Most of the time these parents don't realize until it's too late and the children become adults themselves. As a single parent, it is hard to be both mother and father, but with a little time, patience, understanding, and a lot of love, the problems always seem to work out. The biggest thing I have changed with my children is I tell them that I love them every day.

I have found that the most important ingredients for a happy, wholesome childhood is a good relationship between the child and the parent and/or parents. Every child needs and wants to be told and shown that they are loved and not alone. Children just want someone to listen and understand them. If parents could just ask themselves the following questions and make sure they are giving their children these things, they will find it will make a big difference in their relationship with their children.

- Is my child listened to?
- Is my child cared about?
- Is my child supported?

- Is my child encouraged?

By incorporating these four principals in your family life, parents will find a big difference in their relationship with their children. Children just want to know that their parents care and that they are not alone. It's amazing what a little TLC (Tender Loving Care) can do when given to others.

It is my hope that the following poems and letters, which I have collected from children and adults of all ages, will help other people and let them know they are not alone. I am hoping when parents read these poems and letters, they might think twice about their own relationship with their children and get more involved in their lives.

Ellen Pfaff

DEAR MOM & DAD

SOMETIMES I WONDER

Dad, sometimes I wonder
if you even care about me.

I want to tell you how I really feel,
But I'm afraid of what you might say.
You might say we could talk later,
But I know we would never talk.

I'm afraid of what might happen,
If I tell you how I really feel.

I wish you would listen to what
I have to say.
I'm not even sure what I would say
If you were to listen.

I want to tell you I love you,
But will you tell me you love me?

When you left,
I didn't know what happened.
When I got older,
 I understood more.

I didn't want you to go.
Dad, why did you leave?

Age 18
Toledo, Ohio

JUST CARE FOR ME

You never wanted to be part of my life,
The pain you caused
Left loneliness and strife.

Since I can remember, you never cared,
Each day you tore
My heart into shreds.

I wanted to cry, but kept my feelings inside,
Sometimes you called and said you would come over,
But it seems to me you never tried.

All my life I wanted to tell you, "Just care for me."
I started having hatred feelings towards you,
I finally realized that things you said weren't true.

You never sent cards on holidays or on my birthday,
I couldn't sleep at night,
 if only you could see it my way.

Sometimes I wondered if it was partly my fault.
I knew it wasn't true,
So I brought those thoughts to a halt.

I couldn't understand why you were never there,
My mom always told me
Life wasn't fair.

By Renee Overton
Age 14
Toledo, Ohio

DEAR FATHER

I want to tell you how much you have neglected me.
All of those nights when you were gone,
Half the time you never even told me goodbye.

You are usually gone at least three days out of the week
And I can't stand that.
You try to make up with it by buying me gifts.

I don't need gifts.
I need you to spend more time with me.
I need you to be more of a dad than a father.

By Steve
Age 14
Toledo, Ohio

DAD

Dad, when I really need you,
You're not there.
Dad, when I try talking to you,
You just don't listen.

Dad, it hurts, it hurts me deep,
it doesn't even seem like you care.
Dad, why don't you call?
Are you too busy for me?

Dad, do you even love me?
At times it seems as if you don't.
Dad, I come to you with questions,
But you're always too busy to answer.

Dad, I love you, I need you,
When will you be there?
Dad, I have just one more question,
Do you care?

Age 18
Toledo, Ohio

WHY DAD WHY

Why, that's all I ask,
Why, that's all I want.

Why did you leave me
When I was little?

Why did you say
I wasn't your child?

Why did you make me
Suffer in pain?

While I waited, waited
But you never came.

The only question
I have for myself

Is why I didn't tell you then
What I feel now?

By Gabrielle
Age 18
Toledo, Ohio

BELOVED PARENTS

I want to tell you about my dad. My dad's a cop and he's a good cop. When he's in a good mood, he's really cool, because he's really nice. He only gets mad when I leave after school and don't tell him that I left, or leave a note because he worries about me. But I like my dad because he's always there for me. My dad also coaches my hockey team. When I'm in a bad situation, he will help me through it. Thank you, Dad, for being there for me.

Now I want to tell you about my mom. My mom is always nice to me. She has also helped me through some bad times. Mom, I just want to say I love you, and thanks for buying me clothes, putting a roof over my head, and raising me as well as you did. Thank you for caring about me and treating me with tender loving care. I love you for all you've done for me.

Thank you both. I love you!

By Louie
Age 13
Toledo, Ohio

DEAR DAD

Thank you for all the nice things you do.

Every week on Tuesday,
Even though some of the best TV shows are on,
You always take me to the movies.

I never really tell you thank you
For spending that special time with me.
Dad, I really appreciate everything you do for me.

Thank you!

By Ryan
Age 14
Toledo, Ohio

BECAUSE

It's 9:30. I am home,
But you are not.
It's cold outside,
Inside I am red hot.

Because you are gone, I am sad.
Because you are not home, I am mad,
All because
You are not home.

Because you are gone,
My grades have dropped.
Because you are gone,
These floors I must mop.

Because you are gone,
I am losing my love for you.
Because you are gone,
I am even starting to dislike you,

All because you are not home.
I am missing you,
But you wouldn't know,
Because you are gone.

By Matt
Age 14
Toledo, Ohio

SUPPORT

First life
First death
First true friend
First fight
First performance
First bike ride
First interesting book
First date
First kiss
First breakup

You didn't send me do any of this — why?
All of this is something that makes up who I am.
You didn't share any of this with me.
You had to leave — you said it was for the best,
But some nights I lie awake for hours
Wondering what you are doing,
Why you left, who you love,
And what you are thinking.
Don't you want to share with me?

By Rachel
Age 14
Toledo, Ohio

DAD

Too many years wasted.
You tried your best; you did what you could.
We had the best schools.
You were strict, mean at times.
We didn't understand then, but we do now.
You were alone with four kids.
You did your best.

You were afraid to say,
"Hey, you did a good job," or "I'm proud of you."
 Instead, you said nothing
And assumed we understood, but it's OK.
You did your best.

As we matured and you matured,
You came to know us as adults.
You were able to relate, and you've opened yourself,
Not a lot, but you're trying.
You're doing your best.

You can now say, "I love you,"
Words that we longed to hear as children,
And words that we know you never heard
From your parents.
"I love you" is something we say to our children every day.
We love you, Dad.
You did your best.

Age 43
Toledo, Ohio

DOES WHAT I WANT COUNT

Does what I want count?
To be held through the night when I am sad,
To make my own decision of where to go.

Does what I want count?
To not have to lie about innocent choices,
To finally grow up.

Does what I want count?
Mommy, please let me go,
Love not only who I am,
Trust me only for whom I become.

Does what I want count?
To forgo my own disasters,
To learn from my mistakes.

Does what I want count?
To watch the sun, the stars,
To watch desire burn in my lover's eyes.

Does what I want count?
To be smiled upon by God,
To be handed the moon when I ask for it,
To be saved when I am sacrificed.

Does what I want count?
To be simply held through the night,
To be simply loved,
 To have someone whisper their secrets in my ear,
To not be mocked.

Again, I ask… Does what I want to count?

Age 18
Toledo, Ohio

DADDY'S LITTLE GIRL

The warmth of a father,
You cannot outgrow.
The love from a daughter,
You choose not to know.

We could be together,
To learn, grow, and play,
But this gap in my heart,
Will not just go away.

You said you would be there,
God knows you have tried,
But work comes before play,
And I'm thrown aside.

You always said to me,
I'm the "leading lady" in your life,
Then why aren't you here,
Through my misery and strife?

You can't come to my ball games,
Or watch me grow tall,
But you still consistently say,
I'm the most important of all.

I don't understand, Daddy,
Why aren't you here?
Our lives could be so close,
But you will never be near.

I have not yet begun to forgive you,
For leaving me in my cold home,

But time will heal the pain,
For you're the only father I have known.

When the rain starts to fall,
So do all the tears,
Memories of how you used to hold me,
Help me to overcome my fears.

So instead of hating you,
Sweet father of mine,
We shall work on our pain,
And help our lives to intertwine.

For now we'll set aside the hurt,
And bad memories we'll stove,
Because nothing can overpower
A daughter's love.

By Brittney
Age 14
Toledo, Ohio

DAUGHTER'S FAITH

When life becomes tough and the money is tight,
When the road you travel is too rough,
I'll be here to help you fight.
When the angels begin to mock you,
And the devil start to call,
I'll be here till it's through,
I'll catch you before you fall.

I'm sorry for the chaos I might cause,
I don't need diamonds or a new dress,
We'll take a short spending pause,
But I will never love you less.
If we lived in some dirty alleyway, in a shack,
My belief in you would never lack.
 I will be by your side to stay,
 I'll give you a hug and a smile,
And we'll keep going and never stop.

You can't quit, Mom, it's not your style,
And one day I know,
You'll reach the top.

By Kristy
Age 17
Toledo, Ohio

THE BEST

My mom is the best than all the rest,
My mom takes care of my brother and I the best.

My mom is the best than all the rest,
She goes to work six days a week,
And when we get home,
She always has something for us to eat.

My mom is the best than all the rest,
Even as a single mother with four children,
She manages to keep a roof over our heads.

My mom is the best than all the rest,
When I'm sick at school,
She is cool to come pick me up.

She is always on my side,
Even if she might not know it,
But I appreciate her,
That's why she is the best then all the rest.

By Raysean
Age 14
Toledo, Ohio

DADDY, CAN YOU HEAR ME!

Sorrow holds my heart in my father's hand,
Brutal words escape my mind,
 To only fall on silent lips,
Refusing to roll off my tongue.
"Daddy" is all that is released,
As my tears echo in the silence between us.
Thoughts eager to be heard explode in my head,
Leaving me hurting, grasping for any hope,
Or spark of love.
"Stop hurting me, Daddy!"
I want to scream,
"Love, me, Daddy!"
Fills my heart with agony,
"Don't turn from me, Daddy!"
Releases my tears again.
I reach my arms out to hold him,
Seizing cold air instead.
I watch as again, he walks away,
I hold out my hand, begging him to grasp it.
He doesn't look back.
"Just love me, Daddy!"
Head up, tears streaking down my face.
I finally, for the first time in my life,
Turned my back on him and walked away,
Never to look back again.

By Kristy
Age 16
Toledo, Ohio

THE WORDS UNHEARD

Mom and Dad, it's hard to say,
How I feel everyday.

The things you do with love for me,
Appreciation you may not see.

Sometimes my feelings are hard to express,
But it doesn't mean I love you any less.

It seems you don't think that I understand,
That not everything comes at hand.

I know that I have lied to you,
Guilt I've felt has turned me blue.

Please hold your words from growing violent,
For sometimes my feelings are rested silent.

For a person as emotional as I,
The words "I love you"
May come with a sigh.

By Lindsay
Age 14,
Toledo

MOM

I've always wanted to tell you what I missed growing up because you weren't there. I missed the physical comfort, being cuddled, companionship, emotional closeness, and a strong female role model. I also felt I missed out being a kid and the comforts a mother traditionally provides to her children.

I don't really understand what happened or where you were. I don't remember a lot of my childhood. All I know is you left without a word. Years had passed and I always wondered if I found you, what would I do and what would I say? Then, there you were, a stranger. I found that I had many mixed feelings all trying to get out at once. Part of me wanted to run up and give you a big hug and to forget and forgive. Another part was so angry I just wanted to yell out "Why? How could you leave me when I needed you the most?"

Mom, now many years have passed, and I see you more as a friend than a mother. You weren't there when I needed a mother, but now you have been there when I needed a friend. I still have some anger and with time, this too will pass.

Love,
Your friend,
Ellen

LOST
LOVE

TO MY DISMAY

I stand on the edge that destroys me,
Pulls me apart and leaves me empty.
I am surrounded by darkness that suffocates me,
I am lost amongst the broken souls that see
Right through me.

I am wronged for my wishes and
Damned for my dreams.
I am pushed to go anywhere nobody cares,
It seems that what I am searching is the other way,
Nobody cares, to my dismay.

I follow their path that leads to nowhere,
I do their demands and die in the dragon's lair.
The pain never leaves me, the tears only fall,
The world is so quiet, I hear my call.

I am wronged for my wishes and
Damned for my dreams,
I am pushed to go everywhere, nobody cares,
It seems that what I am searching is the other way,
Nobody cares, to my dismay.

I follow their dreams to be caught in my thoughts,
I whisper to go home, my home I sought.
I pray for them to notice that I am near,
I pray with all my might, they refuse to hear.
So I am wronged for my wishes and
Damned for my dreams.

Age 16
Toledo, Ohio

WHENEVER

Whenever I think of you,
My heart aches.
Whenever I say your name,
My stomach twists.

Though you hurt me,
I hold no grudge.
The pain that was deep inside,
Is buried in the graveyard of the lost and forgotten.

I pray to hold you, kiss you,
Though I know that it will never be,
For apparently
You have forgotten me.

But I want you to know that I'll never forget,
For I could never forget your face, your smile.
I wanted to tell you "I love you" in person
But I feel ashamed
For thinking something was there that's not.

Age 15
Toledo, Ohio

WHAT DID I DO WRONG?

Our love is like a train
That whistles in the night,
From place to place,
With only one light.

Fireworks without color,
Without the noise,
A model that's lost her stance,
The measure of her poise.

My soul can only scream,
Only face the fear,
Of being lost for good,
With only my tears.

I knew it was coming,
Blinded by love,
Ignoring the obvious,
No miracles from above.

My heart has broken,
But no one cares,
As I walk around,
I feel their stares.

I'll walk away,
As if nothing is wrong,
But I can't ignore forever,
My love that was strong.

I guess a kiss was not enough,
My body you have used,

My heart you played with,
My emotions you abused.

My heart will not listen,
As my soul can't understand,
This love I feel,
Did not go as planned.

I'll have to live on,
I have cried,
Tears wasted,
Upon a heart that's died.

By Kristy
Age 20
Toledo, Ohio

MOONLIGHT

I'm lying here in the dark,
With a beam of moonlight
Shining where you should be.

Now, the moonlight only shows
An empty space.

I'm lying here with tears
Looking into the beam of moonlight,
Picturing your face,
The sparkle of your eyes as they look at me,
Your mouth as it smiles with love.

I reach out to touch your face,
And the image disappears.
All that is left
Is the beam of moonlight
Where you should be.

Age 41
Toledo, Ohio

MY HEART

Butterflies filled my heart
When I first looked into your eyes.

Happiness filled my heart
When I saw you across the room.

Excitement filled my heart
When you asked me to dance.

Hunger filled my heart
Wanting more time with you.

Sadness filled my heart
Every time you walked out the door.

Tears fill my heart
When I awake and you're not there.

Age 41
Toledo, Ohio

A WISH

Thy lips receive a gentle kiss,
Whispering a lover's name,
In this world of mortal life,
Someone had gone insane.

Staring upon a sweet face,
A smile full of fire,
A stare that could melt ice,
Secrets of a liar.

A touch that serves its purpose
Has been cast aside,
A caress that carries love,
A love that set abides.

A dying petal falls
Upon the dark of night,
Shines the way to happiness,
A gentle ray of light.

My life was a game
That you got bored playing,
My soul won't stop dying
And my heart can't stop breaking.

The thought of someone holding
My body close to theirs,
The thought that there's a chance
That someone out there cares.

To think there are words
I want someone to say,

All the loving words
That I might hear someday.

God has finally listened
To my painful cry and plea,
Because here you are in my embrace
Where you shall always be.

By Kristy
Age 20
Toledo, Ohio

DON'T YOU SEE THAT I CARE

To stay would be a dream,
To go would be a nightmare.
As I watch you go,
 I cry and scream,
Don't you see that I care?

With all my heart and soul,
I love you.
My glazed eyes stare,
But you walk away.
Don't you see that I care?

What you did wasn't fair,
I stayed by your side,
I held you when you cried.
Don't you see that I care?

I'll love you forever,
Let's never part.
Your eyes aglow, your silken hair,
I kiss your lips, hand you my heart.
Don't you see that I care?

Yet you ignore my plea,
The pain you caused I could not bear.
Your unloving eyes are all I see.
Don't you see that I care?

Love is lost to me,
My poor heart tears,

But I look upon my friend,
I see he cares.

By Kristy
Age 20
Toledo, Ohio

GOODBYE

My heart would not stop dying,
And my soul has run away,
The words of compulsive lying,
And the smiles that just won't stay.
Hot tears ran down my face,
And my breathing came out a sigh,
My life left this place,
When I heard the word goodbye.

The moon stopped glowing,
And the stars all died,
The pain kept flowing,
And my soul just cried.
My heart stopped beating,
I wish I could fly,
My life was fleeting,
When I heard the word goodbye.

I think I lost my being,
And all my happiness,
Lost them without seeing,
With only a goodbye kiss.
What should I do now that you're gone?
I just want to die,
Not live on,
When I heard the word goodbye.

The story is done,
I am empty inside.
I killed the sun,

Nowhere to hide.
My life has ended, I'm through,
I have no alibi,
Everything I said was true,
Until I heard the word goodbye.

Can it be that I could go on
And forget the tender time
We made love upon the rising dawn,
Once when you were mine.
Soon the tears will wash away,
The pain will turn to a sigh,
My smile will return to stay,
On the echo of your goodbye.

By Kristy
Age 20
Toledo, Ohio

CHOSEN ONE

I am lost amongst the many that have loved,
My heart is kept with the others broken,
Led by a steel wolf, we follow behind in chains,
With tears in our eyes and sobs in our throats.

We walk along the jagged road, spilling our crimson blood
And raising our eyes to heaven, we pray for rain
To wash away the stench that evil leaves behind,
But it never comes.

The torment goes on and the pain never ends,
The sickness and death continue,
Some stay brave and some drown in their tears,
Finally putting their souls to rest.

I am one that refuses to give up,
That refuses to stay down in the dirt,
I'll win this war of lost love forgotten
Someday.

I don't care how many lives I'll have to live,
In this slavery of damnation I vow to break the silence
And spill the secrets of the devil,
I will watch them burn in their own fires of hatred.

I will curse the stars in the sky,
For every star lies another broken soul
In search of its freedom,
Within the sun, the moon, the sweetness of life.

The darkness keeps me warm at night,
The lies keep me full,

The hatred keeps me going,
And the death keeps me alive.

I don't know how long I can survive,
But somehow this will end,
The universe shall exist again
Someday.

No one mock my words,
For they are not spoken out of insanity,
They are hopes, truths, and dreams,
Words of wisdom.

My truths are not that of a madman,
But of an old wise woman
Who has been through too much,
Who has seen too much,
And who now knows too much.

I will tell the world of its troubles,
And I vow to save them from harm,
I vow to break the silence,
And let loose the storm.

Bless the gods and give me the power,
To replenish my strength for such a journey,
I am the chosen one.

By Kristy
Age 16
Toledo, Ohio

IN THE BEAT OF TIME

Until I hear your call
The world around will fall,
Upon this heart of mine,
I can feel the withered tears,
A rhythm of falling fears,
In the beat of time.

To feel the rhythm and blues,
Our two hearts seem to fuse,
In this connection we bind,
The nightmares have turned to dreams,
Everything is not what it seems,
In the beat of time.

A restless heart cries aloud,
My pride, my dignity will stand proud
Upon the withered vine,
A scream echoes of sorrow and pain,
A mind screams of sanity now insane,
In the beat of time.

A love will be lost and found,
Another heart will fall to the ground,
Too dizzy to stand in line,
The sweet music reaches my ear,
The beautiful notes soothe my fears,
In the beat of time.

Don't forget to reach a hand
To someone who wants to understand
Something they must find.

Remember that I love you
Is something thought through,
In the beat of time.

Love can be good,
Don't fall from where you stood,
Fate can be kind, walk from where it lies,
From where your heart dies,
In the beat of time.

You can do your best,
Put your soul to rest,
Step off the ragged line,
You could hold him close,
The one you chose,
In the beat of time.

The pain will pass soon,
Bathe in the shine of the moon.
Forget when you were mine,
For my freedom I will fight.
Everything will be all right,
In the beat of time.

By Kristy
Toledo, Ohio

MY ONE TRUE LOVE

A candle burns brightly in a dark room, filling the empty room with the scent of cinnamon, lighting a path for his return. A squeak fills the silence as a rat shreds old newspapers, building himself a new home. Dust covers the rotting wooden floors, outlining his freshly made footprints. Through the open door, a cooling wind blows, making the rocking chair slowly creak back and forth. The fireplace burns brightly and the lopsided table was loaded down with fresh kill. Lost echoes of the sound of laughter free the memories of the two lovers that had once lived here.

The moon smiles upon the crumbling cabin, seeming to understand its loneliness. The stars reassure and the night brings coverage, hiding the tears that fall. He has finally come home.

The creatures of the night seem to follow him as he slowly walks the dirt path, winding his way down to the cemetery below. Clutching the blossoms to his heart, he takes a deep breath and step up, finally confronting his anguished past. The howling of wolves, the moans, the creaks, and all of the night noises fall silent, allowing this broken-hearted man his time of mourning.

He allows the memories to wash over him, surprised that the fist that had been painfully gripping his heart for so long began to lessen its hold. Poised on one knee, he lays the flowers down and bows his head. He can feel the tears held back for so many years flood his eyes. He lets them fall. His shoulders shake and the cries from his heart reach the heavens above.

After the tears are spent, he lifts his head and stares through his red eyes at the resting stone of his one true love. His heart hammering in his chest, he stands raising his eyes to heaven, he imagines her there. A smile touches his lips and one last tear falls. After all these years, he finally has the courage to give her his plecge of love.

"I love you!" he screams it into the night, knowing that wherever she is, she hears him.

By Kristy
Age 18
Toledo, Ohio

PAWN IN YOUR GAME

A heart can be broken when playing a game,
Your heart can be mended, but never the same,
Your soul can be fixed, but some pieces are lost,
Is it worth it when pain is the cost?

Balloons float away into the dead of the night,
A flower can grow with water and light,
A balloon can deflate, a flower can die,
When all is said, a sad goodbye.

Eyes that hold nothing but tears,
A feeling inside letting go all your fears,
A sob an only sound, a thought out of control,
A trigger, a blast, a bullet through my soul.

Blood seeping a silent scream,
All hopes lost, now a bad dream,
The only thing to hold on to
Are the feelings you've stir,
All those things have left and gone,
Now I'm left in the dust for a beggar to pawn.

By Kristy
Age 18
Toledo, Ohio

A TIME SURPASS

The time has come to feed the fire,
Destroy the bitch of undesired,
Hold close the storm of unleashed lust,
Blow away the deadly dust,
Kiss away the tawdry fear,
Whisper sweetly holds me rear,
The smell of flowers reeks the air,
Upon the night her deadly stare.

Black tints the perfect sky,
For one day my heart will fly,
Heartache will surpass my face,
But never will I lose disgrace,
Drop forth blood so red,
You hold no dreams, all is dead,
Echo loudly screams of pain,
My whole mind has gone insane.

A lover's hold means nothing in time,
Never were you only mine,
Lost among the foolish man,
Run away from where I stand,
A kiss of death has struck me down,
I'll lie here dead until I'm found,
Love you? Never shut off the light,
I'll stay here lost through the deadly night,
Call off your wenches or you shall die,
I leave with only one goodbye.

By Kristy
Toledo, Ohio

PAST STAYS IN THE PAST

You break my heart,
With the evil things you say,
We have grown apart,
And I don't have the strength to stay.

I still love you so,
Never doubt me untrue,
I don't want to go,
But I can't stay with you.

You say the glamour is gone,
But you just stopped trying,
You can't fix the wrong,
That left me dying.

There was no other one,
I know that now,
I wish to rescue the sun,
But I don't know how.

Why can't you love me,
Like days gone by?
Why did you blind me,
Then leave me to die?

I only tried to love you,
I thought we would last,
But I guess I already knew,
The past stays in the past.

I heard all the thing,
That people would say,

And how the birds sing,
Then died away.

I heard the truths or lies,
I know not which,
My heart slowly dies,
Isn't loving a bitch.

I wish I could trust you,
I tried to close out the voices,
I tried changing too,
But in life there aren't many choices.

I have no friends,
Or family who care,
I pray the world ends,
Life is so unfair.

I only tried to love you,
I thought we would last,
But I guess I already knew,
The past stays in the past.

By Kristy
Toledo, Ohio

BESTOW THE LIES

Lies bestow a painful grasp
Upon this heart of mine,
Love has no place in life,
No place in unleashed time.

Listen to the words,
Partial truth, partial lies,
The devil wears a cover,
She's hard to recognize.

A voice softly whispers
The words I want to hear,
Love me, kiss me, hold me, and want me,
There's nothing left to fear.

Trapped on stage audience is silent,
Hunger feeds on pain,
The violence grows stronger with every stare,
My life has gone insane.

A lover has no hold
On this soul I keep,
I will never love again,
I will never love so deep.

Do you believe your heartache
Or do you believe the devil's sigh?
Why do you live on, love,
When love left me to die?

I believe no more in happiness,
All that's left is heartache,

When I pressed a kiss to you,
My heart and soul was at stake.

You crushed the dreams that I had left,
I suspect that I should hate you,
But after you held me in your arms,
I can only miss you.

Don't think I'll forget,
Cuz I sure won't forgive,
But I can't thrive on revenge,
I need some hope to live.

A love has no hold
On this soul I keep,
I will never love again,
I will never love so deep.

You see the many tears
As you stare upon my face,
You know the pain you caused,
You lied the love of grace.

Yet you think that it was not a sin,
To lie of love so wrong,
You shall burn in hell for this,
You hear that destiny song.

Think naught of what your heart says,
But of where your heart lies,
Inside the afterlife,
You have no heart it dies.

A lover has no hold
Of someone gone insane,
I will never love again,
I will never embrace the pain.

A lover has no hold
In the soul I keep,
I will never love again,
I will never love so deep.

By Kristy
Age 18
Toledo, Ohio

HIDDEN WISDOM

You say I'm old, and you are not,
But exactly what is the difference?
Oh yes, by looks I'm not a tot,
Is that why you think I'm useless?

My mind goes back to when I was young,
Always doing for the good of others,
But now I am old, and it seems I have clung,
To the dependence of another.

I used to do what you do now,
But time has taken its toll,
It's only my body that's fading somehow,
Not my mind, my heart, or my soul.

They go on living, despite this old frame,
And it is them that carry the key,
To the difference between the young and the aged,
And only death will set them free.

If I only knew then what I know now,
Is something we've all heard,
What good is the wisdom I've gained till now,
If I can't share it with someone to learn?

My experiences are vast, my lessons well learned,
So much I could share if you'd let me,
But how can this be when your eyes are turned,
To only tangible things you see.

Deep inside me, my heart can still feel the pain,
Of rejection from you and your stares,

If you'd only look inside this person who's lame,
You'd find we have much to share.

Yes, the years between us is quite a spread,
And the times have changed, I know,
But down the road you have ahead,
You will reap just what you sow.

By Trish
Ohio

BETRAYAL ON CONSCIENCE

A heart that bleeds black blood
Exists only in a time,
A heart that bleeds red blood
Doesn't exist in time.

A soul that whispers God's prayer
Appears in the air,
A soul that cries
Is afraid of everything unfair.

Eyes that behold
The clouds in the sky,
Eyes that hold
Spirits of the dead that fly.

Ears that pick up
Sounds of hate,
Ears that heard
The cheers of fate.

Lips that smile
At children's play,
Lips that frown
Cuz their smiles won't stay.

Can a time stand
The pain of defeat?
Can a time see
The lies of deceit?

When people scream, "Help me, God,"
Is he really listening?

And if I would raise a plea,
"Help me, God, I'm dying!"

Would he send me an angel
To search for my soul?
Would the innocent child
Be burnt among the coal?

Depression strays so far
From my mind,
The child, the sweet child's corpse,
The devil could find.

Let precious be safe
From his sharp claws,
The devil is hateful,
But God the angel made no flaws.

Keep your child
From ending up dead,
Its sweet innocence appeals
To the devil's appetite unfed.

Turn the sign upside down
To really read the pass,
The color of life fades
In the dying grass.

Forgive me
For this ungrateful turn,
Just leave me, God,
Let my body burn.

My time is up,
The child lives on,
The darkness surrounds,
The sun is gone.

Bound by a signature
From my own hand,
I'll leave and never again
Be seen on land.

Pray for me,
Maybe someone will hear,
My body is empty,
There's nothing left to fear.

Will I ever fly?
Will my life ever feel complete?
Will greed start it all?
But I'll take the heat.

Do I have a choice
To live or die?
Maybe one day
God will teach me to fly.

By Kristy
Age 16
Toledo, Ohio

A Special Way To Say I Love You

POWERS OF A THOUGHT

The parting of our lips
Sets forth a burning fire,
The ashes that are left
Rekindle our desire.

A heart that continues beating
Unspoken promises for someone to keep,
The wind softly whispers
The answers that you seek.

I love the way I feel
When presented by your touch,
Now I know for certain
I love you very much.

The way you hold me close
And say I'm the one
That the moon smiles upon
And I raise the sun.

The only beauty in the universe
Your world revolves around,
You tell me so many things
Without a single sound.

You hold my head up
When a tear escapes my eye,
You kiss away the hurt
And leave me with a sigh.

I shall love you always
Till my dying day,

The devil has called upon me
But for you I must stay.

So with each single kiss
My love for you will grow,
With each single touch
True love shall show.

Beaming from my face
Like a beautiful opened flower,
Covered by each word
And the rays of love's power

By Kristy
Age 16
Toledo, Ohio

MY FRIEND

My friend
My companion
Through good times and bad
My friend
My buddy
Through happy and sad
Beside me you stand
Beside me you walk
You're there to listen
You're there to talk
With happiness and smiles be there
Throughout the years

By Eddie
Age 18
Toledo, Ohio

WORDS OF THE HEART

My heart has raced a thousand miles,
My lips have kissed before,
But never have those beatings
Cried out a lion's roar.

My hand has been gently held
And a caress has touched my brow,
But never has my heaven
Been complete until now.

My thoughts have often drifted
To places lost to me,
My dreams were often spent
In anyone I want to be.

My eyes see naught of hatred,
A virgin's palace I'm kept,
But my mind astute a woman's
And knowing tears were wept.

I am shrouded in innocence,
Though not long everlasting,
The colors show no justice
Depression thou am fasting.

The rotting corpse of peace undead,
"Civility" is called,
I wait inside my crystal tower
For my prince I enthralled.

A lily lifted to gleaming eyes
As it was held in his hand.

I reach to grasp the silky stem
And let the petals fall to the sand.

He touched my face, caressed my cheeks
And told me how I'm fair,
He wrapped me in his warm embrace
And kissed my shoulder bare.

His eyes stripped my senses
And pulled my soul apart,
He listens as I cry
And whispers words of heart.

"Be naught afraid," he says,
"For you know whom I love,"
He holds me close and whispers,
"You, My Goddess Above."

By Kristy
Age 18
Toledo, Ohio

WHERE DO I STAND?

A damask of picturesque flowers
A forsaken dove with a broken wing
I have fallen upon the hardships
I have followed the rocky roads
I have bled crimson drops
And shed many tears
To be where I stand.

I have been broken in a million pieces
I have been called a harlot
Called a naïve girl, but I'm not naïve at all
I lived alone in my own imaginary castle
I was a princess of my own kingdom
And by my side stood an elegant prince
Embracing my hand with his
I have been stepped on
And felt many sorrows
To be where I stand.

Compact pictures fill my mind
Of desolate raindrops
Resting upon soft petals
Mourning the loss of light.
Only to be touched by rays
From God's fingertips
I have been held in a powerful circle
Entwined with sheer bliss
A breeze that intends to never let me go
Has gently brushed me
My mind has been played with

And so has my heart
And my soul has been tortured by the consequence
My thoughts have been left to rot
My dreams have fallen upon deaf ears
Along with my wishes
I have been pushed aside and forgotten
To be where I stand.

God has called upon me,
"You are an angel," he says.
Yet do I know different?
I pray to the Lord to save
My soul and sanity,
My kingdom has crumbled once,
Do I believe in princes and princesses?
I wear the crown and bare the touch,
I kiss the lips and whisper secrets to my prince,
I smile so sweetly, yet I have frowned,
I loved and lost and loved again deeper,
To be where I stand.

With my prince, my savior, my unmasked lover,
Do I fear anymore or do I hear the words that
Chip away at my heart?
No, but "I love you" fills the breath of my dream,
"I love you" brushes tendrils from my eyes
And sets a glow to my face,
My breasts have heaved many troubles,
But now I sigh to unleashed happiness,
True love from my angel of mercy,
Soldier in time, oh my dark knight,

I may stand majestic and virtuous by your side
As an innocent child, but I am not a child,
I am in the flesh of a woman,
My stance is that of maturity
And my heart has occupied
The space of goddesses,
And now I wonder where I stand.

I have searched the sands of time,
I have read all the greatest novels,
Looked through portals of different dimensions,
Reaching for untimely answers
That will put me at ease,
Where do I belong in this vast universe?
The answer follows me,
But it can't be seen by anyone,
There is no respect of life
As he holds me breathless,
As he fills me with his scent
And caresses me with his heated light,
I looked into his eyes and I am lost,
My lips quiver and tears fall,
For there I see his bare soul
And there lies my answer ,
Lost in his eyes,
His kiss smothers by his love,
Held in his embrace, where I belong,
With him for eternity
That is where I stand.

By Kristy
Age 18
Toledo, Ohio

LOVE'S PORTRAIT

Forever has been promised,
A wish to come true,
Could you love me always
Like I could love you?

Happily ever after,
A dream that could perish,
But for right now and always
Your love I will cherish.

Your heart I hold with pride,
Your soul I embrace,
Your lips I praise with a kiss,
My eyes stare upon your face.

The entire thing I feel
Spills forth from my heart,
All that I wish
Is for us to never part.

I stand on my knees
And hold your hand,
I look up into your eyes
To plead my demand.

An angel stares back
And spreads a smile so sweet,
I reveal my heart's secret,
Its rhythms so discreet.

I pledge all the words
My soul needed to say,

And my tears flow freely,
Fears that I cannot delay.

My mind starts spinning,
Repeating your name,
My message reached out to you,
And when I called you came.

You opened your heart
And held me in your charms,
You laid out a canvas
As to paint my portrait.
"To capture an angel," you said.

A beauty so fortunate,
Not with her looks, but her person,
The heart, her soul, her mind,
The way she holds herself,
A true beauty so hard to find.

A kiss was placed upon my lips,
A whisper in my ear,
A loving smile shines light on me,
The words I want to hear.

Now a tricky question
I present to you,
Could you love me always,
Like I could love you?

By Kristy
Age 18
Toledo, Ohio

DON'T FORGET

Please don't forget me,
The girl who handed you her heart,
Please don't forget,
When the time comes to part.
I know I'll see you again,
Once upon a time,
And I will hope and pray
That again you will be mine.

Please don't forget me
Or the love that we share,
Please don't forget,
While you're over there.
Will you still love me
Upon your return?
Will you still care,
Will your love for me burn?

Please don't forget me,
The girl who has shed tears,
Please don't forget
The one who shared your fears.
Who listens to everything you say,
Who does love you so,
The one who begged you to stay,
But understands you had to go.

Please don't forget me
And all the happy memories,
Please don't forget

The loving gentle breeze
That ruffled up your hair
As we held each other close,
Please don't forget
That you're the one I chose.

Please don't forget me,
The girl who dreams
Of you day and night,
Please don't forget
That for you I will fight.
The wind is dying down,
A command from above,
Please don't forget
That you're the one I love.

By Kristy
Age 18
Toledo, Ohio

A GOOD LIFE

My life is precious to me,
My heart has but only one key.

I gave that key to you,
The colors mean freedom like red, white and blue.

I feel no loneliness when you're around,
I stare at you and make no sound.

We're going to marry, you and me,
We'll live in a big white house down by the sea.

Every night we'll watch the sun go down,
And soon our children will be around.

"We have beautiful children," to you I'll say,
And we'll watch them play, play and play.

I tell myself that we'll always be together,
And in spirit we'll live forever.

By Kristy
Age 18
Toledo, Ohio

BE BRAVE, DEAR CHILD

Be brave, dear child,
You're not alone,
Ran away
From the heart of stone.

Be safe, dear child,
Start to fight,
Run away from
The darkness of night.

Come, dear child,
Stand at my side,
Come into the light for
There's nowhere to hide.

Don't cry, dear child,
It will do no good,
You must not hide behind
The darkness of the hood.

Don't run, dear child,
The magic is yours,
You have behind you
The clan of the lords.

Wake up, dear child,
No time to rest,
There's no more comfort
Upon your mother's breast.

Just fight, dear child,
With all you can,

This battle will turn
You into a man.

Laugh, dear child,
Do not cry,
You have saved the world,
No one will die.

Love, dear child,
The best gift of all,
Feel at home and you
Shall not fall.

You're safe, dear child,
No more fights,
You're safe, dear child
From the darkness of night.

By Kristy
Age 18
Toledo, Ohio

SOME PEOPLE

Some people make me mad,
Making hatred ironclad.
So much stress, it gets insane,
Then the stress turns into pain.
Then you turn on other people,
But they are not really bad,
It's just the pain that gets you mad.
To prevent this, you must tolerate,
You must not discriminate,
Against those who make you mad,
Making hatred ironclad.

By Dan
Age 14
Toledo, Ohio

DREAMS

From my heart up real high,
From the ground to the sky.

I'll make my wish and wish it right,
I'll make my wish for you tonight.

I'll wish for peace and for love,
I will get my wish from the stars above.

You brought me in this world one day,
You bring back memories in every way.

1, 2, or even 3, you were always there
For me, from deepest – my heart desires.

Your love and hope raises me higher,
From sunrays to solar beams,
You will always be in my dreams.

By Brandon
Age 14
Toledo, Ohio

NOT THE LAST

Every tomorrow is a day into the future,
Every yesterday is a day into the past,
But every today lived strong and hard,
Makes every yesterday not the last.

If you look forward to tomorrow,
Then today will quickly pass by,
So now you can walk down the street,
With your head held high.

So when you're out and about watching
People come and pass,
Just sit there and say to yourself
Today was not the last.

By Toyneshia
Age 14
Toledo, Ohio

WHAT LOVE IS

Love is when you care about someone
Love is patient and kind
Love is kind and beautiful
Love is a big world of life
Love is special
Love is colorful
Love is brightly beautiful
Love is wonderful
Love is family effort
Love is unselfish and giving
Love is very important to life
Love is truly appreciated
Love is what people want
Love is what people need
Love is what is in my heart and soul.

By Sahara
Age 14
Toledo, Ohio

SENTENCE OF LOVE

I hold a sentence locked within my heart,
Where all my secrets are kept,
Where I hold my dreams of love,
And all my pains that I have wept.

Words that I'd like to say,
But are too scared to admit,
And then you came along,
And a small fire was lit.

A flash of happiness erupted inside,
And then a burst,
I knew that nothing else mattered,
You would come first.

When we first kissed,
And I held you in my arms,
I handed you my heart,
And trusted your charms.

I told you I loved,
My lips have spoken true,
And my thoughts shall never wander,
For they will always be on you.

I don't want to imagine goodbyes,
I do love you so,
I could not withstand the pain,
I could never let you go.

I would never walk away,
For that sentence you have freed,

You have taken the secrets from my heart,
So you are all I'll ever need.

I shall love you always,
Remember that if we part,
I have no secrets for you to know,
I hold no sentence within my heart.

By Kristy
Age 18
Toledo, Ohio

THERE ARE NO WORDS

What am I to say
About this man that
Gently holds my heart
And very being in the palm
Of his soft hand.

What am I to say
Other than he's perfect,
He holds me gently,
Kisses me sweetly
And looks upon me lovingly.

How am I to say the way I feel?
Not in a poem or a song,
Words cannot describe how I love,
I love so deep that my soul aches
For a touch.

A simple touch that awakens
My imaginations to a world
I thought was out of reach,
Now my fingers brush against
The surface ever so softly.

A trail of fire burns my skin
Left by his beautiful lips,
His eyes so deep,
Like pools of sweet chocolate.

And his face,
His handsome face

I hold within my hands,
And kiss lips that seem
To beckon for only my touch.

He has promised me an eternal love
Bound in the eyes of God and children,
Children for me to sing lullabies to,
When lightning echoes in the sky
And fear slips from their innocent eyes.

He has given me all,
My happiness, hopes
And dreams come true.
He has spoken the words
I've waited centuries to hear.

What am I to say
Other than I will love
Only he for all of eternity.
That is all I have to say
For again…
Words cannot express how I love.

By Kristy
Age 18
Toledo, Ohio

OUR FIRST YEAR

Do you know how much I adore you?
Or that you fill my heart
With all your precious smiles,
And promises to never part.

You are my every dream
And my every desire,
With each fluttering kiss,
You fan my fire.

Remember the day we began,
The day we had our start,
The first loving kiss,
The day you stole my heart.

A tender touch in a parking lot,
Oh how you made me shake,
That was just the beginning,
Of all the love we'd make.

A magical evening unraveled that day,
That made my soul soar,
A goodnight kiss,
And I closed the door.

But that was just the beginning,
And now I can't imagine not having you near,
I smile every time I think
That this was the best year.

By Kristy
Age 18
Toledo, Ohio

I PROMISE TO LOVE

A flicker of flame,
A verse to a song,
I knew when you came,
That we'd belong.

The sun with its ray,
The stars with their light,
I told you I'd stay,
Let's make up, not fight.

A dog and its bark,
A cat and its claw,
That ring is my mark,
My love has no flaw.

Candy and its sweetness,
A pen and its ink,
I lose myself in your kiss,
In your arms I can't think.

The moon and its gleam,
The water and its shine,
Your smile how it beams,
And to think you're all mine.

The clouds in the sky,
Then green of the grass,
In contempt I sigh,
Our love will last.

Like the Lord and his heart,
His promises are always true,

I know that we'll never part,
I'll forever love you.

By Kristy
Age 18
Toledo, Ohio

I'VE BEEN THERE

I've been there before
Beyond the grave wall,
I've been there before,
Those legends that fall

A teardrop escapes,
Burns a trail of fires,
A teardrop escapes,
The remains of a liar.

I know how you feel,
But it's not your mistake,
I know how you feel,
Your fragile heart he had to break.

Something confusing,
But what can you do,
Your heart has stopped beating,
We'll pull you through.

The darkness surrounds
Every corner of your soul,
The darkness surrounds
A life that's been stole.

We'll be here for you,
You're our best friend,
We'll be here for you,
We'll be here till the end.

We'll not let you fail
In the fire of hell,

We'll not let you fall,
There's a secret to tell.

We love you,
We'll let you cry,
We love you,
We won't let you die.

I've been there before,
Beyond the grave wall,
I've been there before,
The legends that fall.

By Kristy
Age 18
Toledo, Ohio

FAMILY

MY BOY

Many pieces of my heart are missing,
I'd give my life for my baby.
God, please remember
A heartless mother who
Left her boy caused this.
How could I forgive?
She's left a sweet boy who weeps
For his mother at night,
How could someone that causes
Such relentless pain live?
I love this boy as my own,
For him I will fight
To my victory or to my doom,
I won't give in.
I don't care how long it takes,
I'll fight forever.
She beats him emotionally, mentally,
Physically more of her sins,
Someday, oh God,
Someday we'll be together.

Anonymous
Toledo, Ohio

MY BIG SISTER

On the day of December 9, 1984, you became my big sister. It was a role that no one asked you to take on; it just happened. You and I were not thrilled about this, but you being in the position you were in, you did pretty well. For the past seven years of your life, you were the baby of the family, and you had gotten all the attention. Your sparkly green eyes and bouncy curls impressed everyone.

Then, all of a sudden, there was this new beautiful baby girl, and I was in the spotlight. I took away all of the attention from you. As the years passed and we grew older, we didn't really act like normal sisters did. We never talked or hung out with each other; all we did was flight. We got in competition with each other about who could get the most attention. You've always gotten good grades and you were a great student. I was a cheerleader and dancer. But now looking back, we both had equal love and attention from everyone.

By Michelle
Age 14
Toledo, Ohio

MY DEAR BROTHER

The fear seems to cling
To my body and soul,
My own flesh and blood is dead.
My heart turned to ashes,
I can't see life without you here.
All my spirit is gone,
I can't think of tomorrow without you near.
All I will say is so long,
Goodbyes mean forever,
But for us that's not true,
Someday we'll be together.
With you, dear brother, I am not through,
I want to tell you my heart is full of love,
Every night I pray.
I'll try to find you in the clouds above,
And bring you back to stay.
I love you, dear brother,
Believe it or not,
I'll take care of mother,
I'll give it a shot.
Will you be there when my time comes?
When the angels start to call,
When I feel my last heartbeat,
Will you break my fall?
Wait for me, dear brother,
Don't leave me alone,
I don't want any other.
Wait for me dear brother, I'm full of fear.
Hot tears slip from my eyes,

I wish you were here,
All I can do is cry.
Don't forget me, dear brother,
My heart beats true,
My agony is uncovered,
I love you, dear brother.

By Kristy
Age 18
Toledo, Ohio

TO MY SISTER

Well, here we are, both grown up and leading different lives. It's hard to believe that you're a grandma; time has just flown by. It seems like only yesterday, we were just talking about what we wanted to do when we grew up. What we wanted to accomplish with our lives and what we would do differently when we had our children. How we would never want to put our children through what we had to endear growing up. I believe in many ways we have done just that. We have very loving and caring children. They know we would always be there for them, even if it were just to give them a hug and tell them everything will be all right.

You know I have always considered you to be my best friend. I always thought I could tell you anything and you would listen. Even when I knew you couldn't help, I just needed you to listen. Then as the years passed, I found that you weren't there as much as I hoped. I know you were busy with your own life. But there were times that I needed you. I just needed a hug and for you to tell me everything was going to be all right. I did understand you couldn't be there, but I needed you.

I had recently lost my job and I wasn't sure what direction I was going; I felt so lost. I came to you and just needed you to listen to me, and when you told me that I was a cold-hearted person, I just wanted to die. I felt so alone; I thought everyone would have been better off without me. I really thought about those words. Was I cold to others? Have I not been there for them? You know something? Those words actually have changed me. I want to be there for you and others. I want to listen and try to help where I can. I'm sorry if I came across that way.

You know, losing that job was actually a blessing; it gave me some time to think about what I really wanted to do. No one could really give me answers, but talking to someone out loud really helps to put things in perspective. You know, everyone was put on this earth for a reason; we just need to find our path and follow it. I know where I am going and what I want to do. So you see, you were there for me; I guess that's what you call tough love.

Thank you for being there!

Love,
Your Sister and Best Friend

TO MY GRANDSON

When your parents told me they were going to have you, I cried. What are these babies doing having a baby? I was scared for them and you. Me a grandmother? Not now, I'm too young. ... "Grandma."

I watched my son grow from a little boy to a man, right before my eyes. I cried — where did those years go? I listened to your father say, "My son will know that I love him." Unlike his father, I wept for what he missed.

I was there when you entered the world. I watched you struggle to get here. I watched your father stand by your mother and encourage her to keep going — I cried.

The moment came when I looked at you and held you in my arms. I cried — you looked so much like your daddy. You are so beautiful and perfect — I cried. There is a reason you are here, dear grandson. I will love you, support and always be there for you.

You are in my heart forever...

With love,
Grandma Debbie
Toledo, Ohio

BEFORE YOU GO

I'll love you always,
And I'll miss you forever.
I'm sad that you're leaving,
I'm going to cry when you're gone.
The things that we did,
The laughs that we shared,
No fears in my heart,
Because I knew you always cared.
So go to your journey,
For it's just begun,
Send my love to the others,
From the world beyond.
Someday we shall meet again,
In the heavens above,
Until that day,
I will remember our bond,
And miss you always,
But our memories are strong.

In loving memory of Zazzinell
Great Grandma

By Melissa
Age 15
Toledo, Ohio

LOST COUSIN

It has been six years since you left us, Jack, the day before Thanksgiving. I have forgotten your voice, but not your face or your heart. Scott has two beautiful little girls. He named one of them after you. Jackie is four years old, and Alexandria is almost a year. Jan has one boy named Tyler. He is three years old. Jan, Scott, my mom and I miss you a lot. I bet if those three kids knew you they would have loved you, and if you would have known them, you would have loved them too.

By Jim
Age 15
Toledo, Ohio

TO MY WIFE

I am sitting here pencil in hand, not knowing where to begin. I glance at you staring out the window, and just your presence here makes me feel a tease. When things don't go well for me, when I'm away from you, it's the picture of your smiling face that makes the bad times easier to deal with.

Knowing that when I return to you at day's end, a hug and kiss will be waiting for me. Feeling your warmth as you hold me in your arms and your hands slide under my shirt sends a tingle that makes me feel that everything will be all right.

You're always willing to listen to my troubles and help me to find a solution to problems either at home or outside the home. I hope you will stay with me forever and we always can have what we have now.

With all my love,
Your Husband
Toledo, Ohio

MET HIM

I wish I could have met him
Just once before he passed,
Before they put him under the grass.
I heard stories about him,
He was tall, dark and slender,
I heard he had a heart that was tender.
Fishing we would have gone,
Catching lots and lots of carp,
But, all I can do is harp
And dream of things we would have done,
And had a lot of fun.
If only I could have met him,
We could have been buddies,
Or better yet … Best of Friends.

By Mario
Age 14
Toledo, Ohio

MY SISTER AND ME

From every moment that passes by,
My sister is really great,
But at times she gets mad,
I just feel like running away.

But on some days, she is really great,
And we have a lot of fun,
Just sitting around and joking until
The early morn.

From playing games, jokes,
And clowning around,
Listening to music,
We have fun together.

From every day that passes by,
I know she needs me more and more.

By Stephanie
Age 14
Toledo, Ohio

DEAR BROTHER

I know you don't hear it much,
But I love you.
You know I will always care,
Because of the special bond
Between us we will always share.

When we get in fights,
We will never lose each other,
Or even out of sights,
Cause you're my little brother.

I love you so much, brother,
How much, you will never know,
So, I am very, very sorry,
If I never let it show.

By Brittany
Age 14
Toledo, Ohio

TO MY BROTHER, EDDIE

What happened to you? Why did you leave? Why do you say those things about yourself?

We love you and miss you very much. No matter what you have done or how bad it was, you're still our brother. We want to help and be there for you. Now you're telling us you're dying. Let us help you through this. You say you don't want to burden us, but Eddie, we are family. We love you.

We don't want you dying alone in some hotel in a strange town. We want you here with us. Our family has been torn apart in so many ways, from childhood to adulthood. It's up to us to be there for each other through the bad and good times.

You have a daughter that loves you and just wants to hear from you. The last words she remembers you saying were you don't love her anymore. Eddie, she knows that wasn't true; you really didn't mean it. You just didn't want to hurt her anymore and thought maybe this would be the best way to save her from any more pain. Eddie, you're only hurting yourself staying away from your family. You need us and we need you.

Eddie, you know how there are people that want to say things to each other and discover that it's too late. Please don't be one of those people; come home and be with us. Let us be able to spend the time forgiving and forgetting the past that has come between us.

We love you,
Your loving family
Toledo, Ohio

TO MY SON, ALEX

We may be strangers. We may be worlds apart at times, and there are times when it's hard to accept things we just don't understand. Blind to each other, we only see one side. Some things we may never know, but one thing you should know, "Soul of my soul, heart of my heart," greatest treasure of my life, is what you are, you mean the world to me.

You are growing into a fine young man, and I can't begin to tell you how proud I am of you. You are certainly your own person with your own ideas, and for that, I'm grateful. Once you get over the idea that you "can't" do things and start saying, "I can do anything,' the sky will be the limit for you.

You have always been a great source of pride for me and you have been one of my biggest supporters. Along with being a wonderful and loving son, you are actually my friend. I will love you always. Stay the way you are and be proud of yourself; like yourself and you will go far.

I love you,
Mom
Toledo, Ohio

TO MY DAUGHTER

Kris, when I found out I was going to have a baby, I was so excited. I have always wanted to be a mother. When I was little, people would ask, "What do you want to be when you grow up?" I would always say "a mother." I wasn't sure what kind of mother I was going to be, but I knew I had a lot of love to give you.

I don't think I could have asked for a better daughter. You have been so loving and supportive. I wish I could have been home more while you were growing up. I tried to be open and honest with you. I don't ever want you to be afraid to talk to me about anything that might be on your mind. I want you to know I will always be there for you, during the bad and good times.

I want to thank you for being there for me over the past couple of years. I have been going through some rough times. When you saw I was down, you always did your best to cheer me up. Thank you. I know when you were younger, I wasn't the best mother and I didn't have the greatest patience, but I think over the past few years we grew up together. I have seen you not only as my daughter but also my friend. You gave me a shoulder to cry on many times. Thank you.

I had found myself raising you the same way Grandpa raised me. I'm not saying Grandpa did a bad job. He did his best raising four children on his own. Here I am raising three children on my own. I wanted you to have a childhood; I didn't want you to grow up too fast. I also wanted you to know how much I love you. When I was growing up, I knew Grandpa loved me, but I also know children need to hear it. I had promised myself it was going to be different with my children. I started to see myself raising you the same way, but over the past few years, I was able to change with your help. Thank you.

I want to tell you how proud I am of you. You graduated from high school one year early. I can't say that I wasn't disappointed when you said you wanted to take some time off before going to college. But, now I see you made the right decision. Now you are in your first year of college and you have goals you want to meet. I'm so proud. Thank you for being you.

You see, parents want so much for their children. I guess we try to push our children into something they may not be ready for. I have found the most important ingredients for a happy, wholesome childhood is a good relationship between the child and the parent and/or parents. Every child needs and wants to be loved. They want to hear it, not just be shown. Children need to be listened to, understood and disciplined even, as long as it's not cruel or abusive.

You have helped me to understand that I needed to step back and let you make your own decision, whether it was right or wrong. You told me one time just to tell you that I love you and let you go. You know, that was one of the hardest things I had to do. As parents, we always want to think that our children will always need us.

Now, you have grown to be a beautiful, loving and caring person. It's hard to believe how much time has passed. I remember when you were a little girl sitting on my lap, giving me a hug. I want you to know you're never too big to sit on my lap and give me a hug. I am so proud of you, and lucky to have you. Thank you for being you.

I love you,
Mom

www.ingramcontent.com/pod-product-compliance
Lightning Source LLC
Chambersburg PA
CBHW071608040426
42452CB00008B/1286